Sports Illustrated KIDS

Extreme Sports GOATs

The Greatest Athletes of All Time

Published by Capstone Press, an imprint of Capstone
1710 Roe Crest Drive, North Mankato, Minnesota 56003
capstonepub.com

Library of Congress Cataloging-in-Publication Data is available on the Library of Congress website.

ISBN: 9781669062912 (hardcover)
ISBN: 9781669063094 (paperback)
ISBN: 9781669062950 (ebook PDF)

Summary: How do you pick extreme sports' GOATs? Is it snowboarder Chloe Kim or skateboarder Tony Hawk? Maybe it's BMX legend Dave Mirra. With so many sports, how do you choose? It comes down to stats, history, and hunches. Read more about some of the legends of extreme sports and see if you agree that they're the greatest of all time.

Editorial Credits
Editor: Ericka Smith; Designer: Sarah Bennett; Media Researcher: Svetlana Zhurkin; Production Specialist: Katy LaVigne

Image Credits
Associated Press: dpa/picture-alliance/Sven Simon/Frank Hoermann, cover (bottom middle), Lenny Ignelzi, cover (bottom right), Nathan Bilow, cover (top left), Press Association, cover (bottom left), Vail Daily/Chris Dillmann, 27; Getty Images: Agence Zoom/Christophe Pallot, 28, Agence Zoom/Nathan Bilow, 19, Brian Bahr, 25, Cameron Spencer, 18, 21 (bottom), Clive Rose, 21 (top), Doug Pensinger, 20, 29, Elsa, 14, Harry How, 12, 23, Jonathan Daniel, 15, Matthias Hangst, 26, PA Images/Mike Egerton, 22, Patrick Smith, 9, Paul Kane, 5, Sean M. Haffey, 4, 7, WireImage/Michael Bezjian, 6; Newscom: Icon SMI/Diane Moore, 13, Icon SMI/Tony Donaldson, 16, 17, Zuma Press/Pierre Tostee, 11; Shutterstock: Apostle (star background), cover and throughout, Sagittarius Pro, 10, Sunward Art (star confetti), 4 and throughout, Victor Velter, 8; Sports Illustrated: Erick W. Rasco, cover (top right), Robert Beck, cover (top middle)

All internet sites appearing in back matter were available and accurate when this book was sent to press.

All records and statistics in this book are current through 2022.

Printed and bound in China. 6667

Table of Contents

Words in **bold** appear in the glossary.

How to Pick Extreme Sports' Greatest?

Extreme sports began on the streets and ski slopes. Racing and performing tricks on skateboards, bikes, skis, and snowboards are what make extreme sports fun.

In the 1990s, ESPN created the X Games. That competition brought the best in the world together to compete. Television broadcasts drew even more fans to extreme sports. The traditional sports world took notice. Now, many extreme sports are part of the Olympics too. And the best competitors are getting the attention they deserve.

MOTOREX
DONJOY
ARO
AIRTIME

Skateboarding

Nyjah Huston

Nyjah Huston made history the moment the 2006 X Games started. At age 11, he was the youngest athlete ever to take part in the competition. By then he was already a pro. Huston had signed with his first **sponsor** when he was just 7 years old!

Huston participating in a skateboarding competition in 2008

Huston competing in the X Games in 2019

Huston was on his way to stardom. He practiced all the time on ramps his father had built in their backyard. But his family moved from California to Puerto Rico, which put his skateboarding career on hold.

In 2010, Huston's family returned to the United States. That year, he won his first competition. He has now excelled in skateboarding competitions for more than a decade. As of 2024, he had won 15 gold medals at the X Games. He won six more at the World Championships. And he's a three-time winner of ESPN's Best Male Action Sports Athlete award.

Leticia Bufoni

Leticia Bufoni is one of the most **decorated** skateboarders in X Games history. In 2021, she won her sixth gold medal and twelfth medal overall. That gave her more X Game medals than any other woman.

Born in Brazil, Bufoni didn't begin skating until she was 9 years old. But she was a quick study. She moved to the United States in 2007 at age 14. Three years later, she was named the top women's street skateboarder by World Cup Skate. Graceful and fearless, Bufoni repeated that **feat** for the next three years.

In 2013, Bufoni had her best year ever. She became the first woman to win three gold medals at the X Games in the same year.

In 2021, Bufoni represented Brazil at the Tokyo Olympics.

Bufoni competing in the Olympics in 2021

Tony Hawk

Tony Hawk is one of extreme sports' first stars. His rise to fame in the 1980s put skateboarding on the map. He won his first world title as a teenager. And he held the title for 12 straight years. He became a **household name** in the United States.

Hawk is credited with inventing many moves that skateboarders still use today, including the **ollie-to-Indy** and the **Saran wrap**. And he's the first person to land a 900—two and a half turns in midair—in competition. He pulled that off at the 1999 X Games.

Hawk isn't just a legend on four wheels. He has started several businesses related to skateboarding. In 1999, Hawk debuted his skateboarding video game. It earned more than $1 billion in sales!

Hawk has skated at the White House and on the floor of the New York Stock Exchange.

Hawk completing a 900 at the Globe World Cup in Melbourne, Australia, in 2002

Motocross & BMX

Travis Pastrana

The fastest motorcycle riders in the world compete in motocross events, and the most creative riders perform their tricks in freestyle motocross. Put the two together, and you've got Travis Pastrana. Pastrana was famous for his multiple backflips and daring midair tricks as he set records and amazed fans.

Pastrana won the gold medal in Moto X Freestyle at his first three X Games, starting in 1999. He went on to win the event four more times.

A Rally Car Star Too

Pastrana has set several rally-car records. On New Year's Eve in 2009, he set a record for the longest jump in a rally car. He soared 269 feet in his Subaru Impreza before landing! The previous record was 171 feet, which Ken Block set in 2006.

Jeremy McGrath

Jeremy McGrath is another **pioneer** in motocross. McGrath actually began his career in BMX. That background served him well as he moved on to motocross. As he racked up main event victories and national championships, fans and competitors started calling him the "King of Supercross." He won a total of 17 motocross national titles.

McGrath retired from competition in 2003. In 2009, he entered the BMX Hall of Fame. A year later, he was **inducted** into the Motorsports Hall of Fame of America.

Dave Mirra

BMX owes much of its popularity to Dave Mirra. He was one of the sport's earliest icons. Mirra began competing in BMX stunt riding in 1987 when he was just 13 years old. He quickly began piling up injuries that might have forced other riders to quit. But Mirra was **resilient.**

Mirra competing in the X Games in 2002

Mirra made a name for himself in the X Games. Nicknamed the "Miracle Boy" for his ability to turn a mistake into something impressive, he dominated on the streets and the ramps. He won gold eight times in the BMX Park competition and six times in the BMX Vert. And he won at least one medal in every X Games competition from 1995 to 2009, except for 2006. He didn't compete that year.

Mirra later moved on to rallycross racing. He also appeared on TV shows and in video games.

In 2009, Mirra (center) won first place in the BMX Park Final at the Nike 6.0 BMX Open.

Mat Hoffman

Mat Hoffman earned his living in the air. His tricks and stunts made him one of the greatest vert-ramp riders in history. Hoffman was known for flying more than 50 feet in the air off a 24-foot quarter-pipe ramp. That gave him more time in the air to thrill fans with his skills.

Hoffman has pulled off many amazing BMX feats. He is credited with inventing and perfecting more than 100 tricks. They include the flip fakie—a backflip that includes a backward landing—and the flair—a backflip with a 180-degree midair turn. He is also the only person to land a no-handed 900 during a competition.

Hoffman competing in the 2002 X Games in Philadelphia, Pennsylvania

Snowboarding

Chloe Kim

Chloe Kim became a star at the 2018 Winter Olympics in PyeongChang. But she might have done so four years earlier if not for Olympic rules. Kim was already one of the best snowboarders in the world in 2014. But she was just 14 years old at the time—too young for the Olympics.

Kim remained patient. She won gold medals in the superpipe event at the X Games in 2015 and 2016. She became the youngest X Games gold medalist and the first woman to land back-to-back 1080s in competition.

Then, Kim had her breakthrough performance at the PyeongChang Olympics. Her thrilling run in the halfpipe left all her competitors in the dust. In 2022, she won a second gold medal in the event at the Beijing Olympics.

Kim winning gold at the 2015 Winter X Games in Aspen, Colorado

Lindsey Jacobellis

Simply put, Lindsey Jacobellis is the best snowboard cross rider of all time. The snowboard cross event, in which riders race on a downhill course, made its Olympic debut in 2006. During that race, Jacobellis fell in the final heat. She only won silver. But that just fueled her desire to prove she was the best.

Jacobellis (right) just after crossing the finish line to win gold in the 2022 Olympics

Jacobellis won six gold medals in seven World Championships between 2005 and 2019. But an Olympic gold medal stayed just beyond reach. Finally, after her fifth try, she stood atop the podium at the 2022 Beijing Olympics with her gold medal.

Jacobellis picked up a second gold medal at the 2022 Olympics when she and partner Nick Baumgartner won the mixed team snowboard cross competition.

Shaun White

Shaun White is hard to forget. With his thick, red hair and gleaming smile, he stands out in a crowd. But more than that, he's one of the greatest snowboarders and skateboarders of all time.

The "Flying Tomato" dominated at the Winter X Games. He won 13 gold medals in superpipe and slopestyle. But it's his Olympic performances that made him a legend. He won gold in the halfpipe event in 2006, 2010, and 2018. He **clinched** the last one with back-to-back 1440s.

White winning gold in the 2018 Olympics in PyeongChang, South Korea

White competing in the 2011 X Games in Los Angeles, California

White also became the first athlete to compete at the Summer and Winter X Games. He took gold in the vertical ramp skateboarding event at the Summer X Games in 2007 and 2011.

Skiing

Tanner Hall

The man known as "Ski Boss" is a star on the hill and the silver screen. Tanner Hall won his first gold medal in the Ski Big Air event in 2001. Then he went on to win multiple golds in slopestyle and superpipe.

Hall also helped popularize freestyle skiing with his work in film and television. He's appeared in many movies and series about the sport, which helped fans gain new **insight** into freestyle skiing. It showed them a side of the sport that only the most **elite** skiers usually get to see.

Hall at the 2003 Winter X Games

Sarah Burke

Sarah Burke was the most decorated female skier in X Games history. She won back-to-back silver medals in the superpipe event in 2005 and 2006. Then she went on to win four gold medals in the same event. She also competed in slopestyle.

The Canadian star pushed to get the superpipe event added to the Winter Olympics. And she was successful. The sport made its debut at the 2014 Sochi Games in Russia.

In 2009, Burke won gold in the women's skiing superpipe event at the Winter X Games.

Sarah Burke was the first woman to land a 720, a 900, and a 1080 in competition.

Tragically, Burke never got to compete in the Olympic event. On January 10, 2012, Burke crashed at the bottom of the superpipe during a training run. She suffered a brain injury and died nine days later. Her death shocked the skiing community. But her legacy lives on in the careers of future Olympic superpipe champions.

David Wise

As a boy growing up in Reno, Nevada, David Wise chased his older sisters down the ski slopes. Soon, the other skiers were chasing him. But racing was just part of Wise's skill set on the hill. He was great at freestyle skiing too. In fact, Wise took gold in the ski halfpipe event when it made its Olympic debut in 2014. He backed that up with another gold in 2018. In 2022, he took silver in the event.

Wise competing in the 2018 PyeongChang Olympics

Wise also performed well in the Winter X Games. He's a five-time champion in the superpipe event. That record includes a win at the 2018 X Games, during which he made history. Wise became the first skier to land doubles in all four directions in the same run. That feat helped earn him an ESPY as the Best Male Action Sports Athlete.

Wise at the 2018 Winter X Games

In 2009, Wise became the first skier to land a double-cork 1260. That's three and a half turns in midair! That trick would become his signature move.

Glossary

clinch (KLINCH)—to guarantee a certain result

decorated (DECK-uh-ray-tid)—awarded medals

elite (ih-LEET)—among the best

feat (FEET)—an outstanding achievement

household name (HOUS-hold NAYM)—a person who is known by most people

induct (in-DUHKT)—to formally admit someone into a position or place of honor

insight (IN-site)—understanding

ollie-to-Indy (AH-lee tuh IN-dee)—tipping a skateboard and lifting it with your feet before grabbing the skateboard with your back hand while in the air

pioneer (pye-uh-NEER)—a person who is the first to try new things

resilient (rih-ZIL-yuhnt)—having the ability to recover after something bad happens

Saran wrap (suh-RAN RAP)—tipping a skateboard up on its back wheels and swinging one foot around the front end; often done at the top of a ramp before going back down

sponsor (SPON-sur)—a person or company that provides money to an athlete

Read More

Kenney, Karen Latchana. *Extreme Snowboarding Challenges*. Minneapolis: Lerner, 2021.

Lyon, Drew. *Big-Time Extreme Sports Records.* North Mankato, MN: Capstone, 2022.

Smith, Elliott. *Freeriding and Other Extreme Motocross Sports*. North Mankato, MN: Capstone, 2020.

Internet Sites

Olympics
olympics.com

Team USA
teamusa.org

X Games
xgames.com

Index

About the Author

Brendan Flynn is a San Francisco resident and an author of numerous children's books. In addition to writing about sports, Flynn also enjoys competing in triathlons, Scrabble tournaments, and chili cook-offs.